The DevilStick Book

Todd Strong

Brian Dubé, Inc.
New York

Published in the United States by Brian Dubé, Inc.
Manufactured in the United States of America

Library of Congress Cataloging-in-Publication Data

Strong, Todd
      The Devil Stick Book / Todd Strong.
            p.   cm.
      ISBN 0-917643-07-0
      1. Juggling.   I. Title.
      GV1558. S77   1990
      793. 8'7—dc20   90-34819
                                                                  CIP

First Printing, July 1990
Second Printing, July 1993

CONTENTS

CHAPTER ONE
TERMINOLOGY AND BASICS

Here are some guidelines on how to start playing with your Devil Stick set. Several methods are given with some being easier than others. Try them all. The first two techniques are especially important, as they are the basic patterns from which the advanced moves are derived. The other exercises are good for becoming familiar with the weight and feel of the Devil Stick and can also be developed into more elaborate routines.

Run through the variations briefly, then focus on the ones you like. Do not completely disregard the others, though, as they will prove a pleasant break from too much repetition.

You should work in short blocks of time. Five to ten minutes is fine when you are just starting and don't yet have the bug. Frequent, brief sessions may minimize the frustration some people feel over not mastering a trick right away. If you become frustrated move on to a different exercise or put the sticks away for another time. This will help to lower your anxiety level and may prevent you from learning any bad habits when you are not at your most attentive. Taking breaks also provides a perspective that will make the Devil Stick more enjoyable for you and those around you.

This book is offered in the spirit of joy and wonder at the magic that can be done with the Devil Stick. I have found that the process of learning the tricks is as enjoyable as being able to finally perform them well. Once a trick is mastered try other new ones so that as you become proficient you also remain a beginner. This will prevent your play with the Devil Stick from becoming boring.

A few quick thoughts

When learning a new trick, notice if you are a tongue sticker-outer or a lower lip-biter. For quite a while I could not do certain tricks unless I was biting down on my lower lip. On some days, I concentrated only on not biting that lower lip, doing the trick was secondary. You can use the Devil Stick as a tool to see how you react to new experiences. This makes the Devil Stick an ideal stress-management toy.

On breathing

An important point is to breathe when you play with the Devil Stick. (Actually, proper breathing is important in many of life's activities; but we are trying to limit the scope of this book.) If you don't breathe, you will tire much more easily and quickly, which will shorten your practice time, and may hinder your improvement. Additionally, you will start to turn blue. While the condition is only temporary, it will bother your friends and family if you appear cyanotic.

Two Points From Aikido

A friend of mine, John, who studies aikido is always reminding me of two points, "stay with the experience" and "beginners make large circles, masters make small circles." Somehow they seem relevant right now. Here is a partial explanation.

It is important to concentrate on what you are doing if you want the sticks to dance. Gravity has a persistent habit of ending the dance if you do not pay attention to the Devil Stick. Should your mind wander to paying the rent or wondering what is for dessert, you may find it is gravity and

2

not you who is in control. So, "stay with the experience."

Most Devil Stick movements are subtle, just as most of life's movements are subtle. As beginners we guess at the proper pattern, a bit overwhelmed by all the new activity. Through practice, mistakes, and feedback our patterns get a little tighter. This tightening of patterns can be called 'learning' or 'education' or 'living'. We are all making circles, for the Devil Stick and other things. Beginners make large, jerky circles; masters make smaller, more precise ones.

Here's to mastery.

Sharing the Conventions: A Vocabulary

Ready? Let's set up some common vocabulary terms and conventions.

At present there are no standard names for the different pieces of the Devil Stick set. I use the term 'handsticks' to apply to the two shorter sticks, one held in each hand, and 'center stick' to mean the larger, tapered stick. Since the center stick is the focus of most of the Devil Stick play, I also refer to this one stick as <u>the</u> Devil Stick.

The ends and middle of the center stick are decorated with stripes. These point out important areas on the stick that you need to be able to spot quickly. In addition, these stripes help you locate two other important points, the 'quarters'. The quarter points are halfway between the middle and each end, or one quarter from the bottom and one quarter from the top of the Devil Stick.

Hold the handsticks in front of you with the center stick suspended between them (I know this is impossible, use your imagination). We are now in 'home position' and can share some directions.

Using the mid-stripe of the Devil Stick as the dividing line, we can split the center stick into a top and a bottom half.

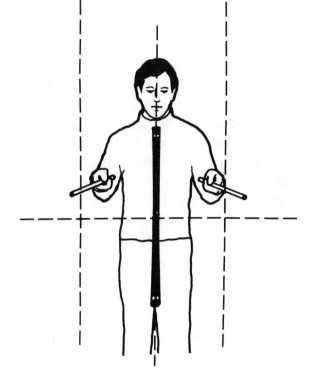

Visualize a vertical line splitting the center stick lengthwise. The center stick now has two sides, the left side that goes with your left hand, and the right side that goes with your right hand.

If two vertical planes were going through your arms and hands you could also divide the space in front of you into three zones. The areas to the left of your left hand and to the right of your right hand make up the two outside zones; the space between your hands is the third zone, the inside. 'Home position' is where you do most of the tricks, here in this inside zone, around waist level.

Finally, imagine there is a wall plane in which the center stick normally travels. This wall plane is perpendicular to your handsticks. We can actually have several wall planes. One close to your hands is the near wall plane. One close to the ends of the handsticks is the far wall plane.

The Grip

The illustration shows what for most people is the most comfortable and controlled grip with the handsticks. Extending your index finger out along the handstick guides your control out to the center stick. Your palm and your extended index finger make contact in two spots giving you two reference points to better feel what is going on at the end of the handstick.

Have the inside tip of the handstick continue about one inch past rather than end in your palm. This lets you grip the handstick securely without having to tightly clamp down on it. Your hand muscles will not tire as quickly.

Other grips are possible. Try different variations to see which is most comfortable and effective for you. However, the majority of people will find that this grip works well as a starting point.

For most of the tricks you should contact the center stick about one to two inches from the far ends of the handsticks.

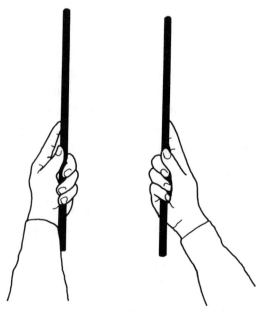

Trapping, Beginning Variation #1

The first technique to try is called 'trapping', 'quick-sticking', or 'doublesticking'. When trapping, both handsticks connect simultaneously on the center stick giving twice the contact area than in other methods for double the control. Once you coordinate your arms in the alternating up and down motion, you should find it pretty easy.

Rest the center stick against your right handstick at the upper quarter point, halfway between the mid-stripe and the top of the center stick. Place your left handstick on the other side of the center stick at the lower quarter point, halfway between the center tape and the bottom. The center stick should be leaning over to the right at a forty-five degree angle.

Keeping the end of the center stick on the ground, use your right (top) hand to push it over so it leans the other way. While the center stick is arcing across, raise your left hand and lower your right to catch it. Your left hand is now between the center stripe and the top of the Devil Stick, and your right hand is between the center stripe and the bottom. Remember, your hands do not switch sides of the center stick, they just change from the upper to the lower half.

The upper handstick makes a ramp for the center stick. Experiment with the position and angle of the handstick and see if you can make the center stick roll towards you or away from you. If you hold the handstick level and at a right angle to the center stick, the center stick should not roll at all. By keeping the handsticks horizontal and pointed straight ahead of you, the center stick will travel straight across in the wall plane without falling forward or backward as you lean it over the other way. Raise and lower the handsticks using your shoulder and elbow joints to keep the handsticks horizontal. If you use your wrists to raise or lower the handsticks, you will change the slope of the ramp and the center stick will spin across in a horizontal arc rather than going vertically straight across.

Holding the handsticks in an open 'V' will push the center stick forward out of the wall plane while a closed 'V' of the handsticks will cause it to fall towards you.

Okay, let us see how things are going. You are trapping the center stick in between both handsticks each time it arcs across. The handsticks are connecting simultaneously. You are finding the 'sweet' spot, halfway between the center tape and each end. The handsticks are remaining horizontal. The center stick is going straight across, staying in the imaginary wall plane. Great!

Now, do the exact same thing, but up in the air this

time. For some reason this makes sense to some people and baffles others. If you want some more hints, read on.

The top hand lifts the center stick off the ground. Set things up so your right hand is the top hand. As you lean the center stick over to the left, also lift it up about two inches. Catch it as before with your left hand on top and your right hand on the bottom. Now the left hand is the top hand. Lift the center stick up about two inches with your left hand as you push it over to the right. You don't need to lift too high to get the center stick in the air. One or two inches will be fine for this exercise.

That's how you start the dance. Whichever hand is on top, and they alternate, provides a little upward lift. Try the exercise again and this time keep the center stick constantly in the air.

You got it? Great. Although it is tempting, don't speed up. Take a deep breath and relax. Stay with the experience. Enjoy it. The Devil Stick is only going as fast as you are hitting it. Slow down and hit it a bit softer. Imagine that you are being awarded style points at the Olympic Games, and you want to show everyone how slowly you can control the Devil Stick. In fact, it wouldn't be a bad idea to stand up straight and maybe point your toes a little. There may be an East German judge out there just waiting for an excuse to give you a low score.

Normal, Regular Devil Sticking
Beginning Variation #2

The second method is different from the first in that you only contact the center stick with one handstick at a time. You no longer have to coordinate your two arms alternating up and down on the center stick, but the release and catch of the handstick on the center stick become much more important.

Start as in the first method with one end of the center stick resting on the ground or some comfortable, level surface. This time as you push the center stick back and forth do so with only one handstick at a time. The contact point is still halfway between the center tape and the top of the center stick. When the center stick leans to the left use your left hand; when it leans to the right use your right hand.

Since you no longer have the bottom handstick to absorb excess energy, it is important to contact the handstick to the center stick just right. Instead of using the handstick to hit the center stick as it approaches, you give with the handstick at the moment of contact. For a split-second, the handstick and the center stick are moving in the same direction towards the outside of the pattern. While in contact and traveling together, use your handstick to slow down the center stick, stop it, and send it back in the other direction.

It is crucial that the handsticks be held in the proper position. If you bend your wrist to slow down the center stick, then the handstick will be pointing down and to the outside, causing the center stick to roll off the ramp created by the handstick. Using your shoulder and elbow joints instead of your wrists to move the handstick to the outside will keep the handstick parallel and pointed in front of you.

Notice that your wrists are held much lower to the ground than might at first be assumed. As you lower them, your wrists should remain in the same horizontal plane of the handsticks. You do not want the handsticks pointing down at the ground.

Okay, it's time to add gravity to the equation. Just as in the first method, as you push the center stick back across, also lift up slightly with the handstick to bring the center stick a few inches off the ground. Each hand now flicks up and across, up and across. Visualize the center stick rising and then falling onto the other handstick where it is steadied, and then flicked back up and across.

This should do it. If you are not now merrily waltzing your Devil Stick about we can try to diagnose some possible problems.

* If the center stick rolls over the top of your handstick, causing loss of control, you are catching it too close to the center tape. Raise your handsticks up slightly to connect at the quarter point, halfway between the middle and the top of the center stick.

* If the center stick travels across without a pendulum type of spin about its mid-point, you may be hitting the center stick too low. Raise your handstick slightly.

* If the center stick whizzes across too quickly to control, you may be hitting it too near the top. Lower your handstick a bit.

The Devil Stick can be controlled without the hand-sticks by using just your open hands. It is tempting to close your fingers around the center stick as it lands in your hand, but remember to keep them open and firm to act like a handstick. This exercise will give you excellent feedback on your touch, which can then be transferred back into your use with the handsticks.

Beginning Variation # 3

Hold the handsticks about a foot apart and balance the center stick horizontally on top of the handsticks. Lightly bounce the center stick up and down on top of the handsticks. This exercise gives you a good sense of the heft and balance of the center stick as well as the action and feel of the handsticks.

Toss the center stick so it flips over one-half turn and catch it again on the handsticks. The right and left ends of the center stick switch places. Flip the center stick back and forth so it spins alternately in both directions. Try full flips, one-and-a-half, or even double flips. Remember to keep this motion as small and subtle as possible. You will not need a very high toss to flip the center stick.

Beginning Variation #4

Rest the center stick on the handsticks as in the previous exercise. Flip the center stick up so it remains horizontal and then cross your hands. As the center stick comes down it will again be resting horizontally on the handsticks but now your arms are crossed.

Most people find crossing one hand over the other natural, but feel awkward reversing the positions. Practice both right hand over left and left hand over right until each motion feels smooth. Who knows? This may be doing something wonderful for your right brain/left brain processes. Try successive crosses with a quick, steady rhythm. For example, on the first toss, cross your right hand over the left. Next flick the center stick back up and uncross your arms. With the third flick up cross your left hand over your right.

A wild move is to cross your hands over the top of the center stick. Flick the center stick up higher and now bring your hands to the outside and up where they cross over your head. Crossed, they continue full circle down and under the center stick to catch it. Done quickly with large arcs from the arms, this always impresses and astounds people.

Properties of the Devil Stick

There are four design features built into the Devil Stick that help you make it dance:

(1) The tubing over the handsticks presents a surface with lots of friction that grabs the center stick.

(2) The tape wrapped around the center stick also provides a surface that grips.

(3) The tapered shape gives a ledge underwhich the handsticks can fit. Being underneath the center stick allows the handstick to lift the center stick up as well as to hit it across.

(4) The taper also puts proportionately more of the weight at each end of the center stick. This weight distribution makes for a slower rotation of the center stick allowing more control.

Effective technique with the Devil Stick requires the successful interplay of these four factors:

PROPER POSITION OF THE CENTER STICK: The center stick should have the correct relationship to your body and field of vision, as well as be properly oriented to your handsticks. Most tricks are done in the "wall plane" that is perpendicular to your vision, passing through the point of contact between your handsticks and the center stick.

PROPER PLACEMENT OF THE HANDSTICK ON THE CENTER STICK: Where the handstick meets the center stick is important. In most moves this is halfway between the center tape and the top of the center stick; in other words, three quarters of the way up from the bottom. You should contact the center stick about one to two inches from the ends of the handstick.

TOUCH: 'Touch' is how the handstick contacts the center stick. An important technique is to let the handstick give as it connects with the center stick. Think of it as a catch rather than a hit. Control is achieved through this split-second catch and then the flick back to the other handstick. It is possible to connect and release either too hard or too soft. 'Touch' is just right.

RHYTHM: The timing and pace of the center stick as it flies from handstick to handstick is the rhythm. When you are beginning; the rule is the slower the better. A breakthrough in learning most tricks is usually preceded by the realization that there is enough time to do the trick; one need not be rushed. The larger the arc of the center stick as it hops between the handsticks, the slower will be the tempo.

On Recovering A Drop

You may find that bending over to pick up a fallen Devil Stick gets tiring. Fortunately, there are several snazzy alternatives to using your hands to recover a dropped center stick.

You know the classy way tennis players roll the ball up off the ground with their racquets? This can be done with the Devil Stick. Place the handstick at a right angle on top of the center stick. Now roll the center stick towards yourself. As the handstick rolls off the center stick, point the tip of the handstick down on the ground and make a ramp up which the center stick can climb. The momentum of the center stick will lift it enough to let you get the handstick back underneath in the starting position.

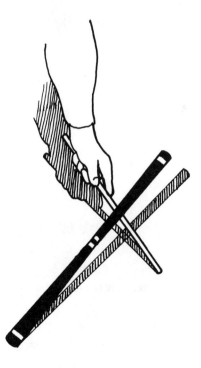

Or, you can place both handsticks on top of each side and end up with the center stick horizontal, on top of them. From this position you are ready to begin again.

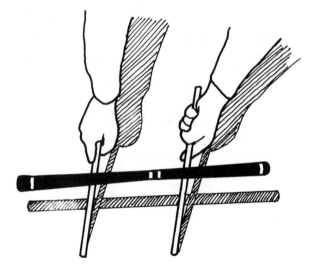

You must still bend over a little for these moves but the extra length of the handstick decreases the distance. Picking up the center stick this way also helps you to think of the handsticks as extensions of your arms.

Of course, my favorite recovery involves no bending over at all. I happen to be lazy. If you are interested, turn to the section on body moves in Chapter Two and read about kick-ups.

About time

Many people are curious to know about the time it takes to learn how to use the Devil Stick. Most people will find that with about 30-60 minutes of time spent using the sticks they will be able to keep the Devil Stick up in the air.

Once this basic question about time is answered a lot of people want to know how long it takes to learn a certain trick or to 'master' the Devil Stick. I think of the Devil Stick as a musical instrument. The more you practice with either, the better you will get. What exactly is meant by mastery? It seems possible to devote a lifetime of study and still find areas one would like to explore.

In answer to the question, "How long?," I must reply, "It depends." People learn and assimilate skills at different rates so there are no set times. However, you will find that ten six minute sessions produce better results than one sixty minute session. This is probably because you are always fresh and sharp when playing in short bursts.

It also seems true that the longer you have practiced and the better you are, the easier it will be to learn new techniques. Sometimes a new trick will be too hard and with no progress being made. Don't think about that trick for a few weeks. When you come back to try it you will find it is easier even though you have not been working on that particular trick. This may be because your mind and muscles are working out the trick while you are not aware of it, or perhaps because you have gotten better at other skills which are related to the trick.

Actually, it doesn't matter how long it takes. There are two types of people who play with the Devil Stick. The first type use it as a toy for fun and relaxation while the second type see it more as a challenge. They will still have fun with it but the primary concern is to master the trick.

If you play with the Devil Stick for fun, it doesn't matter how long it takes to learn a trick. Have fun with it. Pick it up and play with it as often and for as long as you enjoy it. When you are tired of playing, put it aside for another time. You will improve. There will always be tricks you can do and tricks you can't and your most enjoyable time will probably be hovering and exploring between these two. If you learn one trick well and only do that one trick you will soon get bored. And if you only work on tricks you cannot do you will get very frustrated.

If you are challenged by the tricks and make a commitment to master them, then it doesn't matter how long it will take. You will put in whatever amount of time and effort it takes to do the trick. You'll still enjoy working with the Devil Stick and playing around, but if it's the trick you want, you won't be too concerned about time.

Time just happens. It doesn't matter.

CHAPTER TWO
ADVANCED MOVES WITH
THE DEVIL STICK

Introduction to the Advanced Moves

This chapter is the heart of the book. Learning all these tricks will take some time and effort but, in a way, that is the fun part. You can look forward to hours of challenge and excitement. If everyone could perform all these tricks perfectly the first time, there would be no challenge and the Devil Stick would be boring. Initial failure coupled with consistent improvement on all the variations has spurred me on to new patterns I could not have imagined just a few years back. Even now I spend more time on the tricks I can't do rather than the tricks I can do. An appropriate attitude might be, "dropping is learning."

These variations are presented in the approximate order that most people will learn them. Learning the tricks at the beginning of the chapter develops the skills you will need when attempting the harder tricks later on. For example, it would be very difficult to learn singlesticking without first being able to do flips and half-flips well.

Begin at the beginning, but don't wait to perfect each trick before going on to the next. Working on several different tricks and skills at the same time will broaden your understanding of the Devil Stick. The familiarity gained through working on different tricks will have a cumulative effect and will make you a better player.

There is a difference between depth and breadth in learning. Depth is how well you can perform one trick. Breadth is how many different styles and variations you can do. You should try to improve both your depth and your breadth at the same time. Strategies and clues about working with the Devil Stick are scattered throughout these pages. Working on one technique will help with the others.

I find the best way to approach learning the Devil

Stick is with an easy, relaxed, fun attitude. Picking up the Devil Stick briefly several times during the day is more rewarding than one extended session.

Challenge yourself to improve each time you practice and the sessions will stay fresh and exciting.

A recommendation is to practice to music. I am pretty conscientious about my practice and try to put in at least forty-five minutes a day. By turning on a cassette tape recorder, not only do I get background music, but a built in clock, as well. If the practice session is interrupted, I turn the tape off. Right before I resume practice the music is started again. When the tape is over I know that a good forty-five minute workout has occurred without having to watch the clock.

Flips and Half-Flips

When you simply hit the Devil Stick back and forth in the normal pattern, the upper end of the Devil Stick stays up and the lower end stays down. A half-flip turns the top end into the bottom and the bottom end into the top. With your wrist flick up a little higher and impart more force so the Devil Stick spins around 180 degrees before you catch it with the other handstick.

Background Information

The center stick has three different types of motion, all occurring at the same time, as it hops between the handsticks. The first is the lateral side to side movement from hand to hand. The second is a change in altitude, first rising and then falling. The third motion of the Devil Stick is a spinning about its center like a propeller.

The extra spin is what turns the Devil Stick over for the half-flip. Since you are giving the Devil Stick more spin you should also hit it up a little higher so it has more time to flip. Remember to pull your receiving handstick out of the pattern of the spinning center stick, and then reinsert the handstick to stop and catch the center stick again.

Full Flips

In a full full flip each end remains the same after the Devil Stick makes one full 360 degree rotation. The technique is just like the half-flip, flick it higher and with more spin to allow for the flip.

Hints on How to Learn These Tricks

At first try just one isolated flip with either hand then resume the regular pattern. Remember to make this as subtle a move as possible. When you begin to have more control, progress to flipping in a steady rhythm, perhaps every third or second beat with one hand. As you get better build up to every beat with each hand.

Helicopter Spins

An easy, impressive variation of trapping is the helicopter. In fact, many people learn helicopters accidentally from sloppy trapping. If you have not yet practiced too much, you may still have enough sloppiness in your doublestick technique to learn helicopter spins easily.

In a helicopter the Devil Stick changes from vertical to horizontal. Alternate your wrists up and down while trapping so you begin to push the center stick out of the wall plane. While your right hand is pointing up, your left hand should point down. This up and down shift is not perfectly reciprocal. The right hand is dominant for a clockwise spin while the left hand is dominant for a counter-clockwise spin. The other hand still goes up and down a little bit but as support for the strong hand.

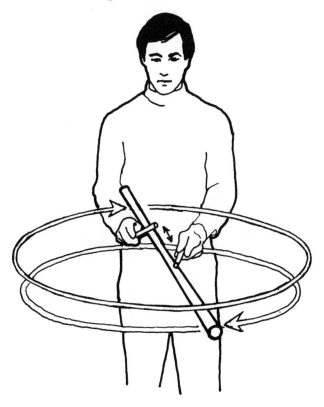

As the helicopter spin becomes flatter or more horizontal, move your handsticks in closer to the center tape for greater control. Contact the center stick out nearer the tips of the handsticks. This will prevent the ends of the nearly horizontal center stick from hitting your hands, which may cause you to lose control. To come out of a helicopter spin back into trapping, merely stop the up and down wrist motion.

You can also go into a helicopter spin using just one handstick at a time. Hold your elbows out a bit wider than normal and use the handsticks to guide the center stick into a helicopter spin. For a counter-clockwise spin your right hand pushes the center stick away from you and your left hand brings it in towards you. For a clockwise spin the right hand pulls in and the left hand pushes out. The handstick stays in contact with the center stick far longer than in the regular pattern which gives you additional control.

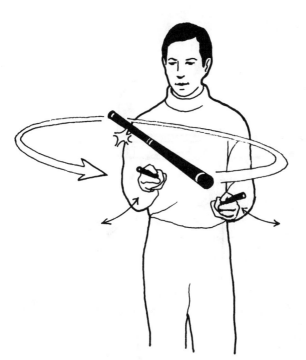

Singlestick Helicopters

Once you get a good spin going, you can maintain a helicopter with just one hand. Aim your handstick to hit underneath the Devil Stick right on the center tape every one-half revolution. Tap the center stick up about two inches so it has enough time to make the half-revolution, and then tap it up again for the next cycle.

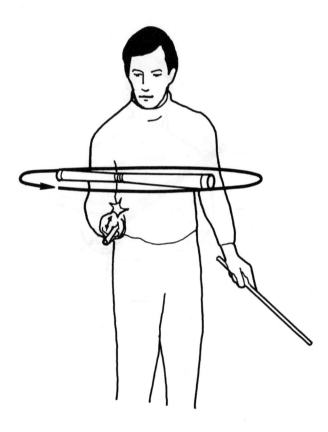

This singlestick helicopter is primarily a coasting move. Each tap hits the center stick up with very little horizontal spin added. This means the Devil Stick will eventually slow down. In order to singlestick helicopter for an extended period, it is necessary to build up to an extremely fast spin while still using both handsticks. When the helicopter slows down, move the handstick away from the center tape back towards the 'quarter' point, and tip it back up to a vertical position to resume the regular pattern.

If the center stick is spinning clockwise, it is easier to use the right hand to begin singlestick helicopters. If the center stick is spinning counter-clockwise, then the left hand should be used to begin. To make the transition from two hands to one hand, lower the appropriate handstick underneath the approaching top half of the center stick, and make the first upward tap. The other handstick should be moved down or to the side, out of the way.

Once you get a controlled singlestick helicopter spin going, it is fairly easy to switch handsticks. During the time between the upward taps, bring the new handstick into position and drop the old handstick out of the way.

Body Moves

Okay, you're getting to be a hot shot with the Devil Stick and you want to add some new challenge and flash to your routine. Well, you can Devil Stick at many different points around your body, not just the front home position. Here are some ideas and hints to get you started.

Under the leg

A good place to begin is under the leg. After your left hand flicks the center stick over to the right, raise your left leg up high enough to fit your left hand and handstick underneath, and on the return cycle connect with the center stick there.

Of course, this can be done with either leg. With fancy footwork and quick hops you can alternate under each leg with every swing of the center stick to get a brisk marching cadence. Watch out for those knees, though. If it doesn't feel too good to do all that hopping about, be content with a slower pace, perhaps every other or every third cycle under the leg.

Behind the back

After hitting the center stick your hand and handstick drop down behind your back to reappear by your waist on the other side of your body. Instead of home position, the action goes on to the side. It is easiest to use the trapping technique when you are in this position.

The hardest part of this trick is to get your hand into position behind your back; once there it is easy to maintain. Five thoughts, (1) throw a half-flip just before you attempt the behind the back move to get more time, (2) point your handstick straight down as you pass behind your back to keep from hitting yourself in the leg or getting entangled in your clothing, (3) move quickly, 4) arch your back, and 5) point your toes. If you go to the left side, point your right toe and keep your weight on your left foot (this will help to arch your back).

Kick-Ups

Rest the center stick in the upper crotch of your foot. The two contact points are at the shin and the base of the little toe. Point your toes up and out at a forty-five degree angle. The center stick should feel secure on your foot. With a quick, crisp motion using your hip and knee joints, swing your foot out to the side.

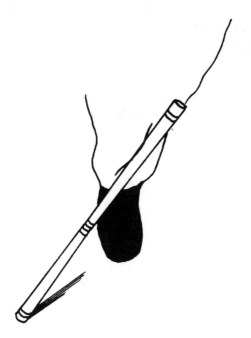

The center stick has enough friction at the two contact points to stay with your foot until it is horizontal, at about knee level. As your foot rises above the horizon, the center stick slides up and off your foot and spins from the outside zone to the middle. The center stick makes one complete revolution while flying into home position where it gets picked up by the handsticks. Kick-ups are a snazzy way to begin a routine as well as a great alternative to bending over to retrieve a drop.

Those kick-ups are static. Dynamic kick-ups are done from the regular routine. Grasp the center stick and hold it almost horizontal but with the tip pointed slightly down. Drop the center stick and catch it in the upper crotch of your opposite foot. To make a clean catch begin with your foot raised and lower it to match the speed of the descending center stick. Once secure, kick it back up. To perform this kick-up during a routine use the handsticks to position the center stick in the same angle that your hand was dropping it. You can also do this from a helicopter spin. The horizontally spinning center stick fits nicely in the upper crotch of your foot.

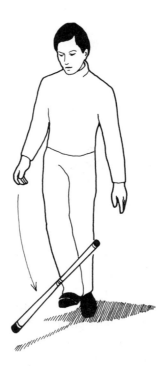

A fun trick is to kick up a Devil Stick in a tight spin and catch it with your foot, where you can again kick it up. Imagine playing catch with your foot. Hacky Sack™ and soccer players watch out.

Singlesticking

Using only one handstick to control the flight of the center stick is not only good for honing your skill but also looks very sharp. Here are some thoughts on a progression of singlestick moves.

With your right hand, send the center stick across with a half-flip. Instead of using your left hand on the next beat, move your right arm and handstick over to the position of the left handstick. Send the center stick back again with another half-flip from your right hand in this new backhand position. This easy back and forth movement with your right hand taking over both the right and left hand positions eliminates the need for the left handstick. Congratulations, you are now singlesticking.

Notice that when the right hand is in the left hand position, you use the outside edge of the handstick. This is like a backhand shot in racquet sports. The tip of the handstick stays in the wall plane of the center stick while moving from the right to the left hand position. Don't worry about the handstick colliding with the center stick. The center stick spinning about its middle will only come in contact with the handstick at the proper two points.

Keep your left hand ready and be prepared to go back into a regular two handstick pattern should you lose control and need to bail out. This will save you many drops and pick-ups.

Try isolated singlesticks until you get the feel, then move on to a consistent every third across singlestick rhythm. That is, every third time you connect with the right hand, you tap a half-flip and use the right hand on the next beat. A cadence would be right, left, right, left, right with a half-flip, right backhand with a half-flip, right, left.

Increase the pace to every other time for a right hand singlestick then finally on to every one.

Use the same progression to learn singlesticks with your left hand. Singlesticks look quite a bit like fencing. A great swashbuckling feeling comes as with either hand you duel with the formidable and elusive Devil Stick.

Singlesticks without the half-flips are slightly faster. To avoid a collision you must bring the tip of the handstick back out of the wall plane of the center stick while moving it to the other side for the next tap. Since you don't gain any extra time from a half-flip, this is a very quick 'out and in' movement with the wrist. While the positioning back and forth is very brisk, the actual tap should be slow and controlled to impart just a tiny amount of spin to the center stick. This contrast between the hurried withdrawal and replacement and the controlled moment of contact makes for quite a challenge. You may want to try contacting the center stick closer to the center tape. This change in position will impart more force to the back and forth motion rather than the spinning motion.

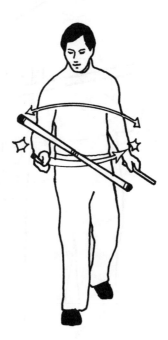

Horizontal singlesticking can be done two different ways. The easier method is from underneath to tap the center stick up, right at the center tape. Since the center stick is balanced at this point, it is fairly easy to maintain the almost perfectly horizontal posture. Should the center stick begin to tip, move the handstick slightly to the tipping side to correct back to horizontal and then return the handstick back to the center tape. This move looks like an upside-down dribble.

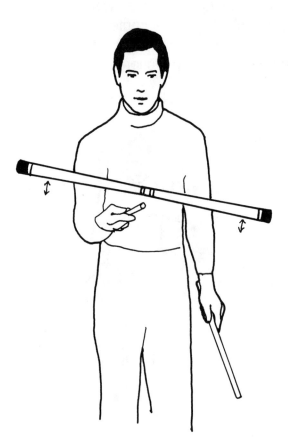

A harder horizontal singlestick move is to change the handstick from side to side after each upward tap. The contact points are again at the quarters, halfway between the center and each end. The center stick now rocks slightly for each tap. Not only does this require moving the handstick back and forth quite quickly, but your touch and sensitivity must be hard enough to tap the center stick up in the air and soft enough to keep it mostly horizontal.

Not as fast but requiring more sensitivity on the receiving end is a full flip singlestick. Again the handstick must be pulled out of the wall plane so it does not interfere with the spinning Devil Stick. The center stick has more momentum after a full spin so the tricky part is to slow it down, control it, and then send it back.

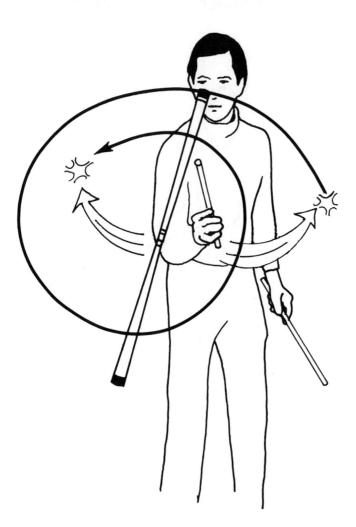

Airplane Propellers

Airplane propellers put the center stick into a tight, vertical spin using only one handstick.

To begin a propeller the right handstick, rather than sending the center stick back with the normal flicking motion, catches, and then pushes the center stick around in a counter-clockwise, vertical rotation. For this first push to start the propeller, the handstick remains in contact with the center stick for a much longer time than for a regular return.

Visualize a clock face in front of you. The tip of the handstick pushes the center stick around in a 120 degree arc from two to ten o'clock, moving counter-clockwise. The center stick now falls away from the handstick as the handstick and the center stick continue their counter-clockwise rotation. Your next connection with the center stick should be just to the right of the center tape under the center stick at five o'clock. The handstick now pushes up and around in a small arc from five to three o'clock to spin the center stick for each subsequent vertical revolution. The tip of the handstick orbits the mid-stripe and comes in touch with the center stick only for this small (five to three o'clock) arc out of every orbit.

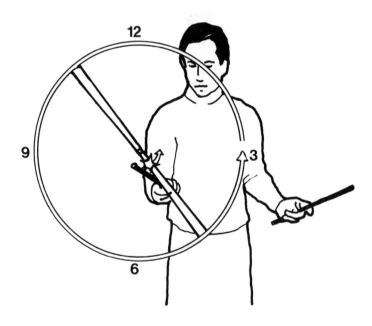

The center stick does not just roll around the hand-stick to make a propeller; the two are not in contact during the majority of the turn. The handstick pushes or taps the center stick around and up for just a portion of each turn.

To reverse direction, catch the center stick at about ten o'clock halfway between the center tape and the top end. Gently cushion and slow the spin, stop the center stick, and send it back clockwise, the other way. A handy hint, to begin or reverse the direction of a propeller, connect on the upper half of the center stick. To maintain an already spinning propeller contact on the lower half.

You can spin propellers in either direction with either hand. First figure out which hand and direction you want and remember, with either hand, clockwise you connect from seven to nine and counter-clockwise from five to three. By coordinating your hands you can switch the propeller from right to left hand and back again. During the free flight time remove the old handstick and insert the new.

47

Slightly trickier is to try all the propeller spin variations using your index finger rather than the handstick.

Crossed Arms

A nifty variation is to try the Devil Stick with your arms crossed. The best way to learn the crossed arms technique is to go back to basics. Try the beginning moves again, but this time cross your arms. Everything will be the same except your arms are crossed, which means you are now using a backhand stroke and the outside edge of each handstick. Try both the regular and the doublestick methods with crossed arms. Don't be discouraged by the fact that you are backtracking with these beginning moves. Consider it a good review and a lesson in humility. Singlesticking also uses the outside edge of the handstick so you might want to practice that for a while, too.

I finally learned the crossed arms variation through a combination of acquiring the coordination and getting very bored with not being able to do it. After many days of the center stick falling forward out of the wall plane to the floor, I just got tired of having to pick it up, and decided to not drop it so often. At the time, it seemed that the conscious decision to not drop was as important as learning the skill. In retrospect, it is hard to say which was the dominant factor, the attitude or the skill.

Comfortable with crossed arms from a floor lift? Use a half-flip to go from the regular pattern into the crossed arms pattern. The extra time of the half-flip allows you to cross your arms to get set up. To get out of the crossed arms position, just use the half-flip and uncross your arms back to normal. Try both right arm over left and left over right.

Chopsticks

Devil Sticks originated in China. A natural variation is to emulate another great Chinese invention, chopsticks. While the grip used is not identical, the similarity of using two slender sticks in one hand to manipulate other objects is too great to not call this move chopsticks.

With your palms up hold both handsticks in one hand so they cross at a point just over your palm. The cross point should be about two inches from the near ends of the handsticks. The outer handstick is on the bottom, being held between the thumb and base of the forefinger. The thumb and forefinger brace the inner (top) handstick, while the other three fingers wrap around both sticks. This grip provides a rigid V-span in which to work the center stick.

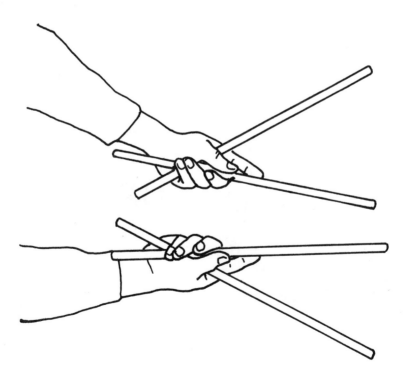

Start by resting the center stick on the horizontal handsticks with your palm up. You can either place it there with your free hand or use the tennis-style roll. Flick the center stick up, pull your hand back, and reinsert the handsticks around the center stick with your palm now facing the inside. Gently rock the center stick back and forth by rotating your wrist.

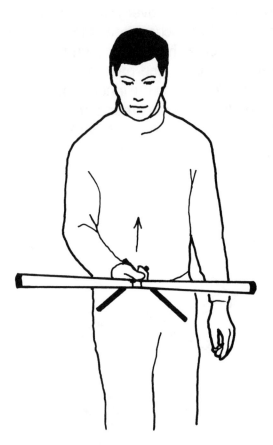

The handsticks trap the center stick around the mid-point as in trapping. Rotate your wrist to change the handstick positions. Be careful now, some people want to rotate their wrist the wrong way. Alternately point your palm up and then to the inside, not the outside. The motion should not feel strained at all. Think of winding a self-winding wristwatch. The handsticks stay almost horizontal throughout the entire cycle. The wrist rotation should be just enough to lean the center stick over the other way. Once it is flicked, you are through rotating your wrist that direction. Reverse the direction of your wrist to again meet the center stick.

Remember when first learning how an open 'V' position of the handsticks pushed the center stick forward out of the wall plane? The open 'V' of the chopsticks grip tends to send the center stick forward and into a helicopter spin. Somehow my hands learned how to straighten out this spin without informing my brain. Most people make this adjustment fairly easily through trial and error, just keep at it.

You like the chopsticks style of Devil Sticking? Try some flips and half-flips. Pull your hand back out of the wall plane to clear the center stick as it spins, and reinsert back into the plane to make the catch.

Double Chopsticks

With your free hand you might want to try a second set of handsticks. Tossing the center stick from hand to hand, you can enjoy a good game of catch.

Or, you can use two center sticks at once. Voila, double chopsticks. Try a series of half-flips with one hand while the other is maintaining a steady rhythm.

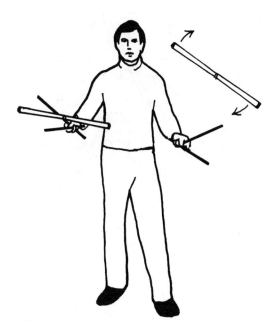

If you establish a near plane and a far plane you can flip both center sticks across at the same time without any danger of a collision.

Stagger the two throws of the center sticks and you get the cadence "throw, throw, catch, catch." This should sound familiar to jugglers as the beginning steps to juggling three objects. With the chopsticks method, it should be possible to cascade three Devil Sticks in a beautiful harmony of juggling and Devil Sticking.

Rollovers

Hold the handsticks in front of you so they are extending horizontally in the wall plane. Move your hands as if they are pedaling a bicycle with the handsticks as the pedals. Spinning the Devil Stick between the two handsticks is a rollover. Another image for rollovers is that of a taffy machine with the Devil Stick being the piece of taffy.

The Devil Stick is mostly trapped between the two handsticks, which keeps it from falling. The lift comes from the near handstick, from horizon to about sixty degrees.

Another way to think of rollovers is to imagine airplane propellers done at a ninety degree angle. In fact, it is possible to do one-handed rollovers.

Rollovers can be done in either direction. To switch directions, have your hands pedal backward instead of forward. Whichever way you're headed, remember to watch out for your chin.

Curls

I had to steal parts of this move from three different people before I could figure out how to do it. 'Lefts' and 'rights' and 'clockwises' and 'counter-clockwises' are all important here so, "pay attention!"

Curls spin the Devil Stick over and under your arm in a type of vertical figure eight pattern. People who spin balls on their fingertips sometimes will curl the ball under their arm. Belly dancers also perform curls with cups of water in their hands.

Start with a singlestick helicopter spin in your right hand, nice and slow. As you look down on it, the Devil Stick should be spinning counter-clockwise. To begin a curl don't tap the center stick up, instead let it land perpendicular on top of your handstick. I like to get the center stick so close to my hand that it is not uncommon for my knuckles to brush up against the center stick.

All you have to do is follow the spin of the center stick around with your hand so the handstick stays perpendicular. After the center stick passes under your arm to the outside of the pattern keep turning your wrist and raise the center stick above your arm. Remember that the handstick stays in contact with the center stick the entire time.

As your wrist turns back to the inside of the pattern start to lower your wrist and raise your elbow. It's strange that arms can twist this way but this brings you back to the beginning and you can try another curl.

I know it's a hard move but basically, that's it. Here are a few tips to make it easier.

Right before I go into the curl I step up closer to the center stick. There is a point where I am looking straight down to see if it has landed in the right spot. To clear my body I have to lean away from the center stick for a short period.

The center stick is so close to my hand that sometimes I can nudge it with my knuckles. This lets me slow down or speed up the spin of the center stick.

To spin a curl only above your arm begin with a clockwise helicopter spin. Instead of a tap bring your handstick up and in just to the side of the center tape. The idea here is to describe a cone with your handstick over head. The handstick is just off center enough of the Devil Stick to lead it around in a horizontal circle.

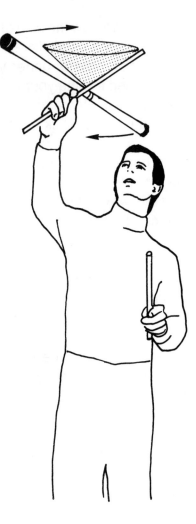

Dual Devil Sticks

The old numbers game, or if one is fun then two should be twice as fun, or as frustrating. How does one control two center sticks with only one set of handsticks? There are several approaches.

The first approach is to use a normal pattern but with a second center stick added. Each stick has its own wall plane, and travels back and forth opposite the other. While the near plane center stick is against the right handstick, the far plane center stick is against the left handstick. Both center sticks pass through the middle at the same time; then the near plane one is against the left handstick while the far plane one is against the right.

Theoretically, this should work. However, don't expect to pick it up in a couple of hours. Several problems must be overcome. The center sticks must go across perfectly straight, the slightest veering out of their wall planes will cause a collision. Because your eyes cannot focus on both points at once, you must rely on the sensitivity in your hands to anticipate the path and the force of the center sticks. To further complicate matters, the lifting leverage of the handstick on the far plane center stick is greater than the lifting leverage of the handstick on the near plane center stick. Flicking with the same amount of force with each hand will lift the far center stick higher.

If you'd still like to try, here are some strategy hints that may help. The lower (or closer to the center tape) you hit the center stick, the less of a spin you impart. The center stick still rises and falls across to the opposite handstick, but does not pendulum as much as normal. This slower spin seems to make the trick easier.

Additionally, your hands need to lift up slightly higher on the near plane center stick. Since the near plane center stick switches right and left hand every beat, both hands must learn a higher-lower lifting rhythm, quite tricky.

Start as in a regular beginning but using two center sticks. They should be lined up on the floor so the bottom ends are in the same perpendicular line bisecting your body.

Dual Propellers

Possibly an easier method to control two Devil Sticks is dual propellers. Begin with the center sticks lying on the floor in the same wall plane in front of you, with a couple of inches separating the ends. Start both propellers simultaneously using the tennis start. I start with the left hand spinning counter-clockwise and the right hand going clockwise. The advantage of dual propellers is that both center sticks can be in the same wall plane without colliding.

You might want to experiment with any of the single-stick variations using two center sticks. Each hand is controlling one stick but they are working at the same time. Whichever method you choose, good luck.

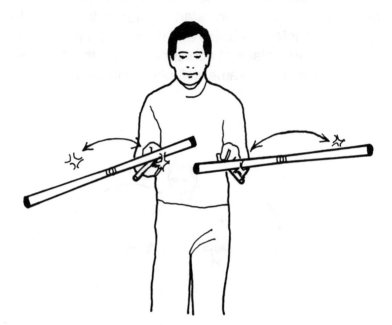

CHAPTER THREE
BALANCING

Invariably, people who spend time with the Devil Stick learn balance tricks. The long, tapering dimensions of the center stick make this an ideal balancing prop. The contrast between the constant motion while Devil Sticking and the absolute stillness while balancing provides a nice range of skills.

While learning different balance tricks you become familiar with the weight and handling characteristics of the center stick, information which will be useful when you go back to regular Devil Sticking. Thus, learning to use the prop as a balance tool will help you become a more well-rounded manipulator in several areas.

The most important point to remember while balancing is to watch the top. Everything else will fall into place (actually stay in place, which is more desirable) with a little practice. All the following explanations are given to justify one point, watch the top.

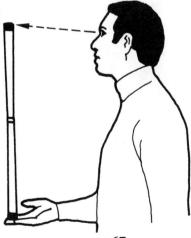

The Goal of Balancing

The goal of balancing is to keep an object still while it is perched on some part of your body. Another way to look at it is to get an object at rest (stationary) and then to keep it that way. The law of inertia tells us that things at rest tend to remain at rest, while things in motion tend to remain in motion. From this law we know that once something is at rest it will have a tendency to stay at rest. So, the hardest part should be to get it stationary. The rest should be easy. Imagine that this well-trained center stick wants to stay put. You just help it out a little bit by adjusting the center of the Earth beneath it.

Actually, what happens when you are balancing is that the center stick starts to lean over and you make a precise adjustment to bring the bottom under the top to keep it vertical. It begins to lean over again, and you make another adjustment to bring the bottom back under the top, and so on. Instead of keeping the Devil Stick absolutely stationary, you are constantly stopping it from falling and correcting back to vertical again, over and over. The trick is to make these adjustments so quickly and precisely that you are the only one who notices the movement. The illusion to others is that the stick is always perfectly still. Make very small, quick corrections to maintain the balance and no one will detect you are out of control for the majority of time.

Watch the Top

Always watch the top of the object. It is the top that must remain stationary. If the top starts to fall then it will bring the whole stick down with it. The bottom can be moved all over the place to get underneath the falling top in order to keep the Devil Stick vertical. This makes sense if you think about it. Things don't fall over because the bottom fell down. It is the top that falls over and eventually brings the middle and bottom with it.

The bottom is connected to the top and is in contact with some part of your body that you can move. Use the bottom as the relay station to control the top. When you move the bottom around you are also controlling the top. Controlled motion of the bottom in a horizontal plane is not that precarious to the Devil Stick. Remember, watch the top, quickly move the bottom under the leaning top to regain a vertical position, and keep the bottom in a horizontal plane.

"An object in motion tends to stay in motion, an object at rest tends to stay at rest." The object being discussed here has 'mass' or 'weight'. The more mass an object has, the more obviously the principle will be demonstrated to us. A larger, longer, or heavier object has more mass and will be easier to keep at rest (maintain a balance) than a smaller, shorter, or lighter one. A pool cue is easier to balance than the center stick of a Devil Stick set because it has more mass.

Also, recall that objects fall from the top down. The more mass or weight there is at the top of the object, the easier it will be to balance. A pool cue with the heavy end up is easier to balance than a pool cue with the light end up.

Newtonian Physics

Objects fall to the earth with an acceleration rate of 32 feet per second per second. When falling, a point on the top end of the center stick is traveling towards the ground at this rate minus some small resistance factor from having the bottom end in contact with your body and friction with the air. Keep in mind this is a measure of acceleration, not of final velocity. If you drop object A, then wait five seconds and drop object B, object A will be traveling faster than object B because A has had more time to accelerate. Therefore, the sooner you stop an object that has started to fall, the slower it will be traveling and the easier it will be to correct. It will not have had the time to get going too fast if you act quickly.

Start to correct a lean by bringing the bottom underneath the top as soon as you detect it. It will be easier for two reasons, the first is because it will be moving slower, as just explained, and the second is because it will not be leaning over as far as it will be in a moment, so there will be less actual distance for which to correct. The farther away the lean is from vertical, the harder it will be to bring the bottom underneath.

Losing and Correcting Balance

Imagine a body walking. Your body loses its balance by putting some of its mass into a forward lean (This mass shift comes from the top of the body by the way.). The body is now falling forward, out of balance. To prevent the head from crashing into the ground, a foot down there at the bottom of the body comes to the rescue by getting underneath the head and regaining the balance. The body leans forward again, begins to lose its balance again, and the other foot comes forward underneath to save the head. Walking is just a series of losing and then correcting the balance of the body, one step at a time.

A Devil Stick leans over, begins to lose its balance, and you bring the bottom underneath the top to keep it upright. It starts to lean over again, and you again bring the bottom under it. Balancing is a constant series of leaning over and then returning to vertical. Unlike walking briskly forward however, the lean can be in any direction. It is closer to a drunkard's walk rather than a determined gait.

Balancing in the Palm of Your Hand

Start with your elbow at your side, forearm extended in front, with your palm up. You should look like you are waiting to accept a tip. Place one end of the Devil Stick on your outstretched palm, steady it in a vertical position, and let go. The Devil Stick will probably stay there for a short while and then fall over. If it doesn't, you are a good balancer.

Try it again and this time make some kind of correction to maintain the balance a bit longer. The grossest correction would be to run forward using your feet to try and keep the bottom underneath the top. A subtler and more practical adjustment originates from the shoulder, elbow, and wrist. Again, the sooner and more precisely a correction is made, the easier it will be. Keeping your wrist in the same horizontal plane will make things easier.

A possible variation is to flick your wrist, send the Devil Stick into a half-flip, and catch it back on your palm.

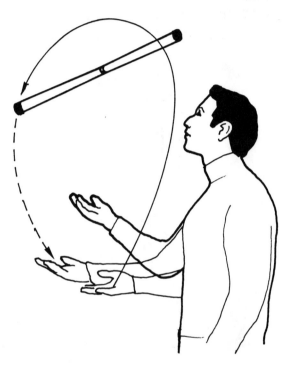

Other Points Around the Body

This same balance
can be done on many
spots around the body.
Try the tip of your finger.

Keeping the balance,
slowly raise your
arm over your head.

The chin and nose work well, especially if you enjoy doing seal impressions.

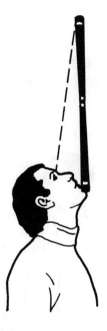

For toe and foot balancing, you should get some shoes with a flat upper surface. Kung fu shoes or ballet slippers work well. You may want to wear several pairs of socks for a little extra comfort. Swing your leg forward a few inches so you can bend your ankle and have your toes pointed down and still be off the floor. Place the Devil Stick on the top of your foot, right at the base of the toes, adjust to vertical, and gently release. It might take longer to learn, but the idea is the same as balancing with your hand.

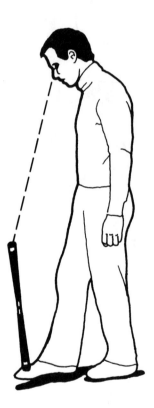

Transferring from One Balance Point to Another

Once you can balance the Devil Stick well at several different points, you can transfer it to these points while maintaining the balance. Use your finger to move it from point to point. The fingertip comes up underneath the edge of the Devil Stick, raises it off the current balance point to become the new temporary balance point. Some possibilities for transferring are fingertip to fingertip, fingertip to chin, hand, or wherever.

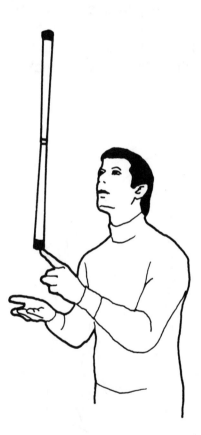

Catching to a Balance

Once you have learned how to balance you can begin the balance from a catch rather than a placement. Hold the vertical Devil Stick about one inch over your foot. As carefully as possible, drop the stick onto your foot and begin balancing. Progressively raise the distance of the drop until the lower end is at about waist level. Now you can drop from a hand balance to a toe balance. Your hand must drop away faster than the descending Devil Stick. Keep the Devil Stick as vertical as possible, and keep your toe right underneath your hand. Some people find it helpful to raise their foot a bit and lower it while catching the Devil Stick to gradually cushion the falling stick and make the catch.

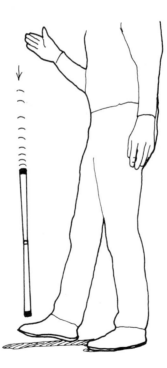

Going the opposite direction, try to make a short hop from your fingertip to your chin. Begin with your finger near your chin and as you gain experience, gradually drop your hand down to your waist. In time a sure flick of your hand up from the waist will have the Devil Stick resting securely on your chin. Perhaps the ultimate in catches would be from your chin to your toe and back up.

CHAPTER FOUR
PARTNERS AND GAMES

Until now, there has not been a lot done with partners Devil Sticking in this country. It is up to us to develop and expand this area of the art. Here are some ideas to help get the sticks flying.

Two Partners Sharing One Devil Stick Set

Two people may each act as one-half of a Devil Sticking partnership. Stand side by side with your inner arms around one another's shoulders or down out of the way. One of you controls the right handstick while the other controls the left. This is a little trickier than if you are by yourself because you no longer have the feedback of the release out of your own hand to anticipate how hard or soft the center stick has been hit. Instead you only have your eyes to accurately judge and anticipate the trajectory. However, with some practice and communication with your partner, you should be able to work it out.

Rather than standing side by side you can face one another. Stand about one arm's length apart with the center stick between you. The advantage here is that you can both use your strong hand if each of you is right-handed. By trading off the handsticks you can combine partners and solo technique in one routine. If one of you tosses the center stick into a high flip you will have enough time to give the handstick to the other person who can make a solo catch.

Two Partners with Two Handstick Sets and One Center Stick

Now you can use the center stick to play catch. Stand side by side or facing one another, and on prearranged signals so there are no surprises between you, pass the Devil Stick. A good pass that is easy to catch is higher than your head with a fair amount of spin. Pass it so it revolves at least one full turn, or even more if you can manage.

Another pass formation is the drop-back, where you pass the center stick up over your head to your waiting partner who is behind you.

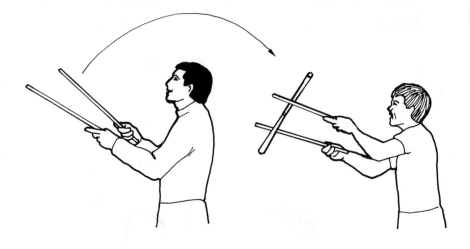

Or, you could stand back to back so the receiver also catches it from over his or her head.

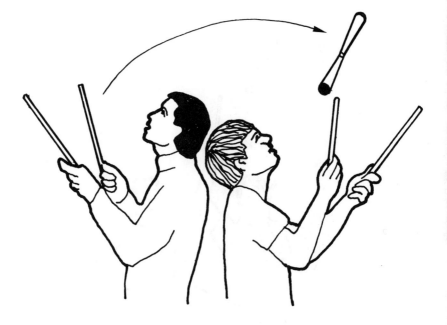

Instead of throwing the center stick away from you, toss it straight up high enough so you can move out of the way while your partner comes in from behind to make the catch. In this move the center stick remains dancing in one location while the people move through the space.

To catch a high toss like this use the doublestick technique. If the spin is clockwise, your right hand should catch the top half of the center stick. If the spin is counter-clockwise, your left hand should catch the top.

Rather than the first player initiating a pass to the second, you can try take-aways. In a take-away the second player steals the center stick from the first. The thief can either face the victim or move in from behind and to the side to walk away with the hot stick. A good thief raises his or her arm up higher than the victim's arm and intercepts the center stick before the victim can hit it.

Of course, the victim here is not entirely helpless. All he (she?) has to do is walk around the thief and steal the center stick back. A pretty routine is the run-around, where both players continually steal the center stick from each other. Player A begins by playing solo with the Devil Stick. On a signal from player B who is behind and to the right of A, they decide to pass off the center stick. With her left hand A sends the stick over to the right and gets out of the way. Player B moves into A's position and picks up the center stick with his right hand. Player A quickly comes around behind and to the right of B to get in position. Now player A steals back the center stick with her right hand while moving back into her original position.

Two Or More Partners Each With A Devil Stick Set

Some of the Chinese Acrobatic troupes perform beautifully choreographed routines with everyone on stage doing the same trick at the same time. This requires planning and practice to synchronize the various moves and the timing for transitions between the moves. The image of a square dance with musical cues and elaborate steps with different partners comes to mind.

Standing side by side and establishing a near and a far plane, you can switch center sticks with your partner. With differently decorated center sticks, a comedy routine could be developed over who wants the blue or the red stick (or 'schtick' in this case), or if one center stick is really better than the other. Of course there would be plenty of switches so everyone could have a chance to compare each stick.

It's possible for two people to pass three center sticks between themselves in a juggling pattern. Because of the length and manner of passing the center sticks (they spin entirely in the wall plane), the normal figure eight cascade pattern of juggling doesn't work too well. Instead, you might want to try the near plane/far plane division so the center sticks don't collide with each other, or perhaps one of you could consistently throw high tosses while the other throws low ones underneath the first.

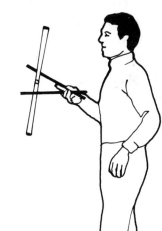

Games with Devil Sticks

There are some games that can be modified to incorporate the properties of the Devil Stick and to challenge the skill of the players.

Egg Toss—Get in teams of two, facing each other along two long lines. After each successful toss, the two lines take a step back to increase the distance between them. The object is to see which team can pass the greatest distance.

Relay Races—The runners must be successfully Devil Sticking to be able to run. If there is a drop, the center stick must be put back into motion before the runner may continue. The center stick gets passed to the next in line before that person can run. This only needs one center stick and three handstick sets per team. The runner always has a complete set and the two lines each must pass a set of handsticks from the previous runner up to the front of the line.

CHAPTER FIVE
BENEFITS AND LEARNING

Playing with a Devil Stick is fun. It's good for you, too. You may experience improvement in any or all of these areas through your play with the Devil Stick.

Eye-hand coordination—You can improve your coordination. Eye-hand coordination is learned through practice. The coordination you gain through practicing the Devil Stick will carry over to other activities.

Timing and Rhythm—You can develop a better sense of rhythm. Proper technique requires not only accurate placement of the center stick in space, but also that the moves be done on the proper beat. The cadence of the center stick as it somersaults to and fro just has to get you in synch with the universe.

Attention Span—You can increase your attention span. The constant challenge and fun of the Devil Stick make you want to keep at it and never put it down. Or, if you do put it down, to get right back to it.

Discipline—You can acquire greater self-discipline. While it is fun to casually play with the Devil Stick, you must make a concerted effort to excel. It takes a commitment of both time and energy to master a new trick.

Self-Confidence—You can gain self-confidence. As your technique with the Devil Stick improves, you'll feel good about your previously undiscovered talent. You should feel proud. After all, you're doing some pretty nice tricks. Show others what you can do. Perform in front of audiences whenever possible.

Different Ways to Learn

This is a "how to" book. Like all "how to" books, it is designed to teach a set of skills. In this case, different ways to manipulate the Devil Stick are being taught. Unlike a lot of "how to" subjects, however, there are no external factors or time limits dictating how soon or how well you should learn, just your own motivation. Most "how to" skills have dire consequences if you don't get it right, the plumbing leaks, the table comes out lop-sided, you don't get the job, or the flowers die. With this skill, the Devil Stick drops (no damage, it's sturdy) and you try again.

Therefore, you can play with your learning. You can not only learn how to Devil Stick, but also learn how you learn.

In this sense the Devil Stick is an educational tool. You can watch your approach to learning new tricks with the Devil Stick and glean some insight into how you approach learning anything new. Being a non-risk activity, isolated from the parts of your life where there are important consequences, you can safely experiment with different learning styles and not be concerned about instant success. If one approach isn't working, you can easily switch to another with nothing lost.

Some people can't wait to try the Devil Stick, but when they don't learn immediately, they quit. Others persist until they gain enough control to shout, "Look at me, I got it!" but they often learn only one or two tricks and put it aside, content to have dabbled. More persistent students may work for hours exploring their own potential and the limits of the toy. Some may invent new tricks. Those with a studious nature might research some of the history of this ancient device.

The important point here is that you don't have to be stuck with just one approach. Have fun and play around with learning the tricks. If you traditionally get discouraged right away, stick around and try practicing when you are alone. If you always rush into things, maybe you can slow down and give some thought to how you will approach the next session.

Think of this book as allowing you a chance to learn a skill, the art of the Devil Stick, and also a chance to learn about how you learn, meta-learning.

The Devil Stick fits into the broad category of things that people like to spin, twirl, and swing. There are many toys, tops, yo-yo's, Hula Hoops, and Frisbees, that also reflect this basic fascination people have for spinning objects.

Many performers rely solely or in part on the mesmerizing quality of spinning objects to delight and amaze their audiences. Baton twirlers, rope spinners, club jugglers, rifle drill teams, even percussionists spinning their drumsticks between beats are all utilizing the collective sense of fascination we share in circles. Our nervous fingers and exploring minds often find ways to spin and twirl even the most mundane objects. The cop on the beat swinging a billy club, basketball players who spin the ball on their fingertips during time-outs, and night security guards swinging the keys on their key chains all share in the cyclical nature of the orbiting cosmos.

As the aikido master said, "We are all making circles, master and beginner alike."

How big are yours?

CHAPTER SIX
HISTORY — ORIGINS AND PROLIFERATION

There are two questions that must be answered when dealing with the history of any object. What is the origin of the object, and how did it spread?

Origin

The Devil Stick fits into the category of simple toys. The pieces that make up the Devil Stick are basic, three sticks. The simple design of this toy is comparable to the simplicity of the yo-yo, top, or ball. Like all of these toys there is a wide range of difficulty one can attempt, from beginner to expert. And like most of these basic toys, the exact origin has been lost to history.

The common stick was such a powerful tool for early mankind it was looked on with reverence and awe bordering on mystical worship. Will Durant, in the first chapter of Volume I of the *Story of Civilization*, describes the development of tools that primitive peoples took from nature:

> Many tools lay potential in the plant world that surrounded primitive man. From the bamboo he made shafts, knives, needles and bottles; out of branches he made tongs, pincers and vices; from bark and fibres he wore cord and clothing of a hundred kinds. Above all, he made himself a stick. It was a modest invention, symbol of power and authority, from the wand of the fairies and the staff of the shepherd to the rod of Moses and Aaron, the ivory cane of the Roman consul, the *lituus* of the augers, and the mace of the magistrate or the king. In agriculture the stick became the hoe; in war it became the lance or javelin or spear, the sword or bayonet.[1]

Sticks have the potential for so much power it is easy to see how people came to hold them in awe. For someone to be able to make a stick hop and jump and seem to dance to their every whim as with the Devil Stick would indeed be spellbinding. One can surmise that a superstitious, primitive people might regard such a device as a devil's stick and believe the person demonstrating such control had made a pact with the spirit of evil. Fortunately, this is not the case. The actual reason for the name 'devil' stick is much more mundane. It comes from the Greek word which means to toss across, but more on that later.

One of the earliest written records on this toy shows the Devil Stick to be over two hundred years old.[2] Most likely the toy has been around for much longer, and may be thousands of years old. Certainly the materials and technology to make Devil Sticks have been available for thousands of years.

In China, the Devil Stick is known by another name, 'hua kun'. 'Hua' means flower or flowery and 'kun' means stick or rod, so 'hua kun', the flower stick. Two pieces of thin bamboo are used for the handsticks while the heavier and larger center stick is wrapped with bright strips of calico cloth and has colorful pom-poms on each end. Some of the spinning movements of this brightly colored center stick are reminiscent of a flower, opening up in bloom, hence the name. (More on how a Chinese 'flower stick' came to be called a Greek 'toss across stick' and an English 'devil stick' later.)

The flower stick was used as a toy or prop in a type of folk dance. The players would sing and dance while tapping out a beat and performing various tricks with the flower stick. There is even a singing rhyme, 'ta hua kun', or hitting the flowery stick. ('Ta' in Chinese means to hit or to strike.) Another folk toy that has singing rhymes and dance movements associated with it is the jump rope.

What probably happened is that the better players of the flower stick game were asked to add to the gaiety at festivals and special events by demonstrating their skills. In this manner the common folk toy and dance was elevated to the status of a professional performing art. One early record describing a flower stick performance appears in the book, *An Account of Great Attractions in the Imperial Capital During New Years Celebrations*, written in 1758 during the Ching dynasty.[3] In this account we see the flower stick was performed along with many other attractions during the festivities.

This same elevation in status to a performer's prop has occurred with other common toys. Baton twirling students around the country are delighted to display their skills marching and performing in parades and pageants. Frisbee competitions in which the better players show their expertise are held both locally and nationally to promote the sport and allow the players an opportunity to share their knowledge. Some of the better Frisbee players have turned professional. They tour the country putting on shows with their flying discs.

We are fortunate today to witness the revival of the flower stick and other circus and juggling acts in the People's Republic of China. On October 1, 1950, the first anniversary of the Chinese Liberation, Chairman Mao Tse-Tung and Premier Chou En-Lai witnessed a private performance of circus related arts in Peking. From this performance a national program supporting the circus arts and acrobatic troupes was begun.[4]

This program has proven to be quite successful. Circus troupes are not only sponsored by city, county, and provincial governments around the country, but the demand for this ancient type of entertainment is so great some troupes are sponsored by rural communes, large industrial concerns, and the army. Today over eighty such troupes are active all over China.[5] There is a standard set of acts taken from the Chinese tradition of the "one hundred entertainments" which most troupes master and then go on to specialize in one particular style or prop. The Nanking troupe specializes in toss juggling, the Canton troupe specializes in balance, etc.

In 1958 the Shenyang troupe began working on an act incorporating the flower stick with folk music, dance, and acrobatics.[6] Today the Shenyang troupe is considered to be one of the finest performing troupes of the flower stick in the world.

Through the ages, performers of the flower stick have passed on a saying describing the four necessary qualities one needs in order to excel. "Make your body agile, hold your elbows steady, make your every movement neat and clear cut, and devise countless variations."[7]

Proliferation

Before we get into the spread of the flower stick to the west, we must briefly look at and note the similarity of the flower stick to another Chinese toy, the 'kouen gen' or in this country the diabolo. 'Kouen gen' translates loosely into the hollow bell. It, too, consists of two handsticks which are used to manipulate a third center stick. For the hollow bell the center stick is shorter and the taper is more pronounced. In fact, the ends of the center stick of the hollow bell are actually two hollow bamboo wheels about three inches in diameter. The 'stick' is more of an axle connecting these two wheels.

A string connecting the two handsticks is placed

under the axle of the center stick and is used to spin the hollow bell in a manner somewhat like a yo-yo.

In English the hollow bell is called a diabolo or sometimes the devil on two sticks. Note the similarity in names between the devil stick and the diabolo. One can actually think of these as two versions of the same toy. For one version the motion is a hitting back and forth, and for the other version the motion is a spinning one.

On With the Story

Most likely the flower stick came from China to the western world sometime around the mid-1790's or the early 1800's. At that time the governments in Europe were very interested in developing increased trade with the Orient. While Europeans were allowed to land and trade in Shanghai, a southern port city, the interior of China was declared off limits to foreign traders by the emperor.

Lord George Earl Macartney was head of an English expedition in 1794 whose purpose was to try and set up an embassy in the interior of China for eventual improved trade relations with the entire country. Though the trip was unsuccessful, the party was allowed to stay only 67 days before being asked to leave by the emperor, the members were given views of everyday life of the Chinese that few other Europeans had seen.[8]

That there was interest in the Orient among Europeans is evidenced by the fact that not only did Lord Macartney publish his journal of the trip, but several other members of the expedition also published their diaries and journals. As an interesting aside, one of the party members whose book was published was to later gain some notoriety for a similar type of expedition journal, the Mutiny on the Bounty.

In 1796 Adrian Houcksgeet Van Braam was a recorder for a similar embassy mission to try and establish a trading base for the Dutch in China. Again, the mission was ultimately unsuccessful but there were several journals published in Europe by various trip members describing life in China.

A few years later some French missionaries stationed in China began sending back accounts and artifacts of Chinese life to a friend of theirs in the French government, M. Bertin. In 1812 he had collected enough information to publish his book, "*La Chine en Miniature*," or "*The Chinese in Brief*," a guide for the French on the everyday life of the Chinese people.[9]

It is uncertain which of these people had the greatest influence on the popularization of the flower stick and the hollow bell. There is a good chance they all mentioned them and the word was spread. In 1813 a handbill advertising a Berlin theater's evening show announces "the performance of Chines stickplays by Medua and Mooty Samme."[10] Though the name flower stick or hollow bell is not used here, we can safely assume that Europe had been introduced to both.

All these ambassadors, missionaries, and government workers were well-educated. Indeed, they had to have been in order to have held their positions of authority and responsibility. From the tone of the journals one also gets the impression that they were highly chauvinistic, believing themselves and European culture to be much superior to the 'heathen chinee.' One can easily imagine their desire to share the artifacts of China, but the mood is of sharing oddities and novelties rather than serious cultural objects.

In this mood there is no need to maintain the original Chinese names for these items, instead they chose to apply their own names. Being educated people they spoke

Greek, a mark of erudition. So, the toys were given new Greek names.

In Greek, the term 'diaballo' means to throw across. It comes from a combination of 'dia' meaning across or through (as in the diameter of a circle, a line that crosses a circle), and 'bolla' or originally 'ballo' which means to throw (we get the modern word 'ballistic' which means to throw from this Greek root).

Probably the two toys both went by several different names for a while, Chinese stickplay, Chinese yo-yo, diaballo, hua kun, kouen gen. In time 'diabolo' was retained for the spinning version of the Chinese sticktoy while the hitting version of the sticktoy was rendered into English as the Devil Stick.

It is interesting to note that the term 'devil' itself also is derived from this Greek diaballo meaning of to throw across. A secondary meaning of diaballo in Greek is to slander or to traduce, to talk ill about somebody. If someone does not talk right at you but out of the side of his mouth about you, in essence, that person is slandering you. In political jargon this slandering of an opponent is called 'mudslinging' or tossing mud around.

This slanderer (diabolos) shows up in the early Greek Bible. When Jesus Christ is fasting for forty days and forty nights in the desert, he is tempted by a diabolos. (Matthew, Chapter Four, Verse One). From this general slanderer who is an evil spirit the term grew more specialized to mean the evil spirit, Satan, the one who can speak no good. In Spanish we have el diablo, in French le diable, in Italian il diavolo, and in English the devil.

From the original Chinese flower stick, through the Greek language as the toss across stick, we now have in America the Devil Stick. Whatever you want to call it, it sure is fun.

FOOTNOTES

[1]Will Durant, <u>Our Oriental Heritage</u>, vol. 1 of <u>The Story of Civilization,</u> (New York: Simon and Schuster, 1954), p. 12.

[2]<u>An Account of the Great Attractions in the Imperial Capital During New Years Celebrations</u>, trans. Zhan Gao (Peking: Peking Press1978), p. 10.

[3] Ibid., p. 10.

[4] "The Great Circus of China" (performance program, Canada 1982), pp. 5-6.

[5]Ibid., p. 6.

[6]Ibid., p. 6.

[7] Ch'u Pan She, <u>Chun-kuo tsa chi i shu,</u> trans. Zhan Gao, (Shanghai: Shanghai Wani, 1959), p. 86.

[8]Lord George Macartney, <u>An Embassy to China</u>, (Hamden, CN: Archon Books, 1963).

[9]M. Bertin, <u>La Chine en Miniature</u>, (Paris: Nepuen Librairie, 1811).

[10]Ricky Jay, "Letter to Editor," <u>Juggler's World</u> 35 (March 1983) : 23-24.

CHAPTER SEVEN
VARIATIONS ON A THEME

I hope you enjoy this book and find it useful in learning how to play with the Devil Stick. Please do not think that this covers all aspects of the Devil Stick or all the possible tricks. Remember the part of the wise Chinese saying reminding us to 'devise countless variations.' There are as many tricks that are not covered here as there are imaginations to devise them. Currently, I am working out how to pass the Devil Stick behind my back.

One obvious field to explore for new ideas and tricks is the world of juggling. Try adapting three-ball juggling tricks to the Devil Stick. There is a convention among jugglers to share their tricks so it should not be too difficult to get some pointers.

The other part of the Chinese saying is about "making your every movement neat and clear cut." Which tricks seem to follow others well? How is your overall presentation? Consideration should be paid to your posture and your delivery as well as your ability to master the trick. Does it look nice? There is till much to explore and perfect within the field before going on to other areas.

Once you get the basic pattern internalized, look around and see what else is handy that might work as a Devil Stick. Just about any long, slender object will do.

Tennis racquets work very well and add a new flavor to the art of Devil Sticking. Used tennis racquets are fairly inexpensive at local thrift stores. If you are willing to risk a possible drop, you may completely psyche out your opponent and change the outcome of a match as you casually toss your all-star, ace, alloy racquet around with some handsticks as part of your warm-up for the finals at Wimbledon.

For performers a great, universal comedy object to use as a center stick is the plumber's helper. You can get a lot of laughs in your routine with this inexpensive, commonplace tool.

There Must Be Some Way to Use This in Swan Lake

The converse to using different props as Devil Sticks is to use the Devil Stick in a field other than what is covered here.

You might want to incorporate the Devil Stick into a dance. Some of the variations and moves would look very beautiful set to music.

There is a wealth of ideas in the art of baton twirling. The center stick is shorter than most (not all) batons but can certainly be used the same way. A baton twirling friend says the Devil Stick is particularly well suited for body rolls. Picture a combination baton twirling and Devil Stick act that needs no prop change.

Or you might want to use one or more center sticks as a staff for martial arts exercises. One woman carried a Devil Stick set with her when riding public transportation at night. This gave her a chance to practice her technique at transfer points and made her feel more secure knowing she had some obvious self-defense handy.

It is possible to use a counter-point rhythm when doublesticking to tap out different beats. One hand strikes the bottom, then that same hand hits the top before the other hand for some syncopation. Perhaps a musical Devil Stick could be made into a percussion instrument.

In summation, this book is a start. If my modest effort is successful you will become intrigued enough to carry through on some of these ideas, or others you may come up with. There is still a world of possibilities to explore and nothing to stop you. Devil Sticks are inexpensive, portable, durable, harmless, and fascinating. A great hobby.

Even if you should master all the tricks in this book there are still new vistas. After six years I have not exhausted all the avenues I would like to explore. Every time I pick up the sticks there is something new, which keeps me a constant beginner.

Isn't that nice?